I'm With The Team

The story of my summer with the Harvard football team

By Zachary Malott
With help from Daddy

This book is dedicated to everyone on the Harvard football team and coaching staff. You have all gone so much out of your way to make my experience with the team so really wonderful. My special appreciation to Coach Crook, who made this all possible and Barbara in the Athletic Office for everything you have done for us. Also, I must thank Coach Murphy who has done so many wonderful things for us and made us welcome at the practices. Everyone has made me feel like family and has been so wonderful to me and I am so forever grateful.

Beat Yale!!!

All my best……. Zachary

Once upon a time one summer, I got to spend a lot of time with the Harvard football team. The football teams name is the Crimson. Harvard is a big university in Boston where I live. Harvard is the oldest college in America.

Football was born here, way back in the year 1874. The first game ever played was here at Harvard on May 14, 1874.

Harvard Stadium

Harvard Stadium is where the Harvard football team plays games and one of two places the team practices. It was built in 1903 and the very first game played here was on November 14, 1903 when Harvard played against the team from Dartmouth University.

The scoreboard was also used here in Harvard for the very first time ever anywhere on November 30, 1893.

Harvard's scoreboard at night

Almost every college has a football team. So, the teams from colleges are grouped together in little groups with other colleges that they play against during the football season. Harvard is in the group known as the Ivy League.

The football team practices all the time. During the winter a big bubble is put up over the football field so the field can be used year round.

The team practices in the stadium and on a big field that's next to the stadium. The football field in the stadium is not real grass. It's a special turf, like a carpet that's made like grass.

When the team has a game coming up on a field that's real grass, which some football fields still are, they practice in the field.

The Harvard team practices on the grass field next to the stadium

I love to run around on the field in the stadium when the teams not using it for practice. They have a big ball that I really like to play with and I push it all over the field.

From one side all the way to the other

Sometimes I have the whole football field to myself to play. Daddy and I run around and make believe we're playing football or play tag.

I know to get that football into the end zone, I can almost hear the crowd cheer!

Sometimes when I go to the football field, I see my friend, Isaiah. He plays for the pros and even has played in the Super Bowl.

He runs really, really fast and I get to chase him. Sometimes we race each other from one end of the football field all the way to the other.

Isaiah played for the Harvard football team and is the all time leading tackler for Harvard.

I go to football practices all the time. I am unofficially on the Football team, I wear number 36, and I get to be in charge sometimes of filling up the water bottles.

And dumping out the water bottles after practice

There I am friends with all the players and coaches on the team. They all know me by my name. Sometimes I have to give them football advice too.

Or help them with getting the footballs and
Other equipment

And help them warm up

Sometimes, I stand on the sidelines with the other players

Or sit off by myself and guard the equipment

Sometimes I like to be right in the action

Or off to the side

Sometimes I play catch with the guys

Sometimes I sit on the water cart

or sometimes I like to sit in the water cart

and I like to sit with the girls when we drive back and forth to the field

I like all my new friends at Harvard

Coach Murphy is the head coach of the Harvard football team and is really good at it. He has set lots of records and my team usually always wins. He has been super nice to me and even gave me a football signed just for me by him for me to have. Coach Murphy has been the head coach of Harvard's football team for fifteen years and has led the Harvard football team to many championships.

Being the coach is important because the coach runs the football team and along with his staff makes all the calls to what plays to run.

Coach Crook is another great person. He is our Offensive line coach and he is the one who first took me into the locker room and introduced me to Coach Murphy and he gave me all kinds of neat Harvard football stuff. Coach Crook has been very, very wonderful to me and he's one of my good buddies.

Barbara works in the football office and is a super, super person. She has done so much for me. Her job is very important and she takes care of lots of business stuff for the team. I love to go and see her when I go to the practices and give her a great big hug.

I like to watch the practices

And giving instructions to my workers

And I work hard to help, even cleaning everything up when practice is over

But, most of all . . . .

I love to go to the Harvard football games.

The very first football game I ever went to, was a Harvard game. It was a night game and all the lights were on in the stadium. It was on September 19, 2008 when Harvard played Holy Cross at Harvard Stadium.

At half time I got to see the Harvard band perform and the team went to the locker room to talk about the game

Coach Murphy talks to the quarterback about plays, because Harvard was behind and needed to win

And Harvard kicked off to start the second half of the game

and I cheered for Harvard to win

AND HARVARD WON 24 -25

Each year the Harvard Crimson football season starts in September and the team plays every Saturday until late November. In late November, Harvard plays their biggest rival, Yale University. The Harvard-Yale rivalry is one of the most famous in college history.

Harvard 2008 Football Schedule

Sept. 19	Holy Cross
Sept. 27	at Brown
Oct. 4	at Lafayette
Oct. 11	Cornwell
Oct. 18	Lehigh
Oct. 25	at Princeton
Nov. 1	at Dartmouth
Nov. 8	Columbia
Nov. 15	at Penn
Nov. 22	Yale

In the old days of football, players wore leather helmets to protect them

Nowadays, there is lots of stuff to protect the players from getting hurt. Helmets have changed lots since the old days. A new kind of helmet that's even safer was invented by a man who went to Harvard.

One day the whole team signed a football for me,

and gave me a helmet, and I even got a game winning football
used in the very first football game I went to from the team captain. I've gotten jersey's, t-shirts, posters, books, footballs, and tickets and lots of neat stuff. It all goes up on my bookcase, so I can look at it and have it when I get older.

I even go to the away games and here we played Brown University
and it Rained the whole game

And I cheered for Harvard the whole game

And stayed close to my team during the game

But I was glad to get back to Harvard again

And back to practice

And back to running around the stadium

And dreaming about one day when I'm a famous Harvard football player

And making my way into the end zone to score lots of touchdowns for Harvard

But for now, I'll just enjoy being the unofficial water boy and being part of the Harvard family, a wonderful group of great people.

And study my law books, and get ready for law school

Harvard University Gates
THE END